ABUNDANT STRENGTH

A CAREGIVER'S PRAYERS

LYNN H. WYVILL

Developmental Editing: Stacia Fleegal
Content Editing: Ann F. Hammersmith
Proofreading: Shayla Raquel, shaylaraquel.com
Cover Design & Interior Formatting: Melinda Martin, melindamartin.me
Author Photo: John Berry

ISBN: 978-1-7333545-1-6 (paperback)

CONTENTS

WHEN I NEED PEACE

A Caregiver's Gratitude

A Prayer to St. Jude for the Elderly

About the Author

PREFACE

Abundant Strength: A Caregiver's Prayers came as a surprise to me. I was writing my first book, *Nature's Quiet Wisdom*, while I was caring for my elderly parents. Even though they didn't live with me, their care consumed most of my time and energy. There were many days when I felt lost, lonely, discouraged, and inadequate for the job.

I was at Mass one Sunday, and during silent prayer, an idea popped into my head, like the sun peeking out from the clouds.

There was no voice. No angels sang, but the call was strong: Write a book of prayers to the Lord, pouring out everything I carried in my heart about being a caregiver.

The Bible was the source of my inspiration, particularly the Psalms, my favorite book in the Bible. After I read, I would pray, talking to God in my own words. In the stillness, I felt the presence of the Lord beside me. These quiet times, sometimes only a few minutes, brought me great comfort.

This book reflects my caregiving experience—the doubts, fears, joys, and the trust that God is always with me.

I am not a theologian, priest, or member of a religious order. I am a daughter who did her best. These words come from my heart, inspired by the Lord.

My hope is that this book of prayers will console and strengthen you, lead you to rely on the Lord's grace and guidance, persevere in this most important work, and know that you are never alone.

May the Lord bless you and your loved ones.

Lynn

A Caregiver's Psalm

Lord, you are always with us
When we are at our best and our worst
To comfort and guide us.

Lord, bless the impatient with your peace
The weary with strength
The frustrated with tenacity
The discouraged with courage
The inexperienced with wisdom.

Bless the fearful with confidence
The sleepless with rest
The sorrowful with serenity
The grieving with consolation.

Make our faith in you unshakable
Our trust unwavering
Our love for you unceasing
Our hope unending.

WHEN I AM WEARY

Why Have You Called Me?

Why have you called me, Lord, to be a caregiver?

I am not prepared.
I don't want the responsibility.
I don't want to sacrifice time I'd like for myself.

I'm not the right person for this work.
My heart isn't big enough.
My spirit isn't generous enough.

Why have you called me to be a caregiver?

I'm angry with Mom and Dad because
They won't listen,
Discuss their situation, or
Admit they need help.

Mom and Dad are angry with me because
I'm forcing them to confront
Their aging and profound change.

Please don't ask me to be a caregiver, Lord.

My answer to your call should be
"Your will be done," but I am
Struggling to say those words.

But I do say them and ask that you
Make my eyes sharp like an
Eagle's so I can follow your path.

Make me strong like
Saplings that push between
Rocks to find the sun.

Make me courageous so
I can walk through the
Frequent storms of caregiving.

You are placing Mom and Dad's
Care and well-being in my hands.
Make me worthy of your sacred trust.

DIFFICULT TRANSITION

Mom and Dad refuse to move
To a place where they can live
A safe and healthy life.

When I talk to them, Lord,
Forgive me for angry, frustrated words.
Please give me tender ones.

Give me empathy to understand
Their sorrow at leaving their home
And facing the realities of old age.

Give them wisdom to recognize
The need to move instead of my
Forcing them to do it.

Our whole family is afflicted, Lord,
With the pain of growing older.
Ease our suffering.
Grant us peace.

CALM MY SEA

Lord, I am being tossed on
The rough, desolate sea of
Caregiving that threatens to
Overpower and sink me.

I am struggling with so many
Decisions, questions, and
Responsibilities. I can't
Hold on much longer.

Lord, calm the sea for me
Like you did for your apostles.
Walk on the water toward me.
Speak your reassuring words.

Climb into my boat,
Take the rudder, and
Save me from drowning.
With you, I will not be afraid.

FINDING THE RIGHT WORDS

I have many words, but my
Tongue fails me. My words are
Inadequate to soothe Mom and Dad.

If I speak of their sadness,
Am I encouraging them to be
Stuck in their valley of tears?

If I talk of blessings,
Will they think I haven't
Heard them or I am unfeeling?

Lord, when sadness settles over them,
Help me ease their fears and
Give them hope.

Supply me with comforting words
To console Mom and Dad.

THEIR NEEDS FIRST

Mom and Dad sacrificed for me,
Put my needs ahead of theirs.
Now I must put their needs
Before my own.

When I should go grocery shopping
And they want to go to the bank,
Make me a willing giver
To them of my time, Lord.

Remind me insurance forms can wait.
Taking Mom and Dad to lunch and
Walking with them among the roses
Means more for their health and happiness.

Remind me, Lord, that this time is short and
What is important is to spend time with them and
Make their remaining days full of love and joy.

(

What Hearts Say

Help me, Lord, to hear not just
The words my parents are saying
But to listen for what is in their hearts as well.

In the whisper "I'm not hungry" is
The exhaustion of staying alive.

In every "I don't want to live here" is
The frustration of losing control over their lives.

In the cry "Doctors aren't helping me" is
The fear that they will never get well.

In the weariness of "Let me sleep" is
The yearning to be undisturbed.

Make me swift like a rushing river to grasp
The deep meaning, feelings, desires, and pain
Beyond their words.

Make me still like a turtle resting in the sun
So I listen attentively and
Understand what their hearts are saying.

Pray without Ceasing

You are my shepherd, Lord.
You guide me to green pastures.
You protect me in the dark valley.
You give me courage.

When Mom and Dad are hallucinating,
I pray for the words that will soothe like
A cooling breeze on a sultry day.

When they hurt,
I pray I can ease their pain like
Smooth stones that warm my hands.

When they barely touch their food,
I pray I can feed them like
The rain you send to nourish the soil.

When they don't remember what I just told them,
I pray for patience like
The bird that joyfully repeats its song.

When I have to shout because they can't hear,
I pray for fortitude like the
Tireless ocean tides.

When I have so much responsibility for them,
I pray for energy like the
Hummingbird whose wings never tire.

When Mom and Dad are sad and confused,
I pray for a spirit that can warm them like
The sun on a cold winter day.

On the most difficult days, Lord,
I pray for hope like crocuses that
Bravely poke through the ice-crusted earth to bloom.

WHAT DO I SAY?

Lord, I am lost in the
Night with no moon or
Stars to guide me.

What do I say when Mom has fallen,
But they refuse to call an ambulance?

What do I say when Mom asks,
"When can I go home?
When will Dad get better?"

I can't say, "You can't live alone.
No one will get better.
You can never go home."

What encouraging words can I use to
Give them hope and
Lift their spirits?

Grant me caring and honest words
That lead us out of the
Frightening night into your light.

NEVER GIVE UP

I am weary. I don't want to
Think about aging anymore or
Manage the details of Mom and Dad's lives.
Lord, I don't want to do this work.

I haven't given up, but
I'm tempted and I'm struggling.
I haven't given up, but
I'm complaining and I'm stumbling.

Too many times, too many days,
I fall under the weight of this cross,
Unable to cope with one more
Chore, phone call, or crisis.

Disregard my complaints,
Overlook my imperfections,
Forgive my selfishness,
Ignore my pleas to lift this cross.

Look with mercy on my flaws.
Don't give up on me, Lord.
Quench me when I am parched,
Withering like a plant in the scorching sun.

Shade me with angels' wings.
Refresh me at the river of your grace.
Baptize me with trust in you.

SWIMMING IN THE SEA OF CAREGIVING

Care for myself first,
Friends and aging experts say,
So I have the strength to
Care for those who gave me life.

How do I do that, Lord, when they are
Frightened and need reassurance,
Discouraged and need me to listen,
Heartbroken and need consoling now?

I can't tell them no or to wait
When they need so much but ask for so little
Because they don't want to be a burden.

I'm caught in a rip current of
Endless needs, unending care,
Desperately trying not to drown.

Rescue me, Lord, so we can sit
On the shore together and I can rest
My exhausted body and weary mind.

Just a few minutes to pray with you,
To catch my breath, to restore my spirit
So I can swim gracefully in the sea of caregiving.

FORGIVE ANY BITTERNESS

Lord, I'm doing the work
Of caregiving that you've asked me to do.

But I'm not always the
Cheerful giver you want me to be.

Too often, I resent that so much
Is being asked of me.

I'm angry that my retirement plans
Have to be set aside.

Thanks to your grace,
These feelings are fleeting.
My prayer is that all Mom and Dad see is
My love and care for them.

Lord, forgive me.
My hope is that
Any good I do
Far exceeds any bitterness.

My Help Is in the Lord

I turn to you, Lord, with
My *big* problems and try to
Cope with the small ones alone.

I don't want to bother you when you are
Busy helping others with problems
Far more serious than mine.

So I work harder and will myself
To be stronger so I can manage.
But I can't.

Humble me, O Lord.
Teach me to ask for and accept
Help from you and your people.

Help me recognize the hands
Stretched out to me are your hands
Answering my prayers to you.

MORE LIKE MARY

Lord, when you visited your friends,
Mary sat at your feet
Captivated by
All you had to say.

Martha busied herself caring for you.
She wanted help, but you
Said Mary had chosen the
Better part: listening to you.

I've mostly been like Martha:
Busy with visits, errands, and paperwork
For Mom and Dad.

I need to be more like Mary:
To stop what I'm doing and be
Attentive to all you have to teach me.

But I won't always be able to stop
And listen. So please talk to me as we
Walk together, caring for Mom and Dad.

Renew Me, Lord

Lord, you preached,
Healed the sick,
Fed the crowds,
Worked miracles.

When you tried to sleep,
The apostles woke you
To save them from the storm.
And you did.

You must have been weary, Lord,
With so much work, with so many
Clamoring for your attention and
Asking for so much.

Lord, you gave yourself willingly,
Totally, but always took time
To rest, to be alone, to pray.

Guide me to follow your example.
Still my racing mind.
Slow my pounding heart.

Call me, Lord, to your garden
Of lush palm trees, fragrant jasmine,
And a cool pond to pray with you.

WHEN I NEED COMFORT

Alone

The old folks sit
In their rooms, the hall,
The dining room,
At the front door.

Alone.

No matter how often we visit,
They endure many hours
With no one to talk to.

They must feel abandoned as
Family, friends, and spouses pass away,
Knowing that death is
Close for them too.

Some have no one to visit or call,
Celebrate birthdays and holidays, or
Lavish love and attention on them.

No one to replace worn clothes and shoes,
Buy the lavender hand lotion they like, or
Bring daisies to brighten their day.

Embrace the elderly, Lord, and
Bring people into their lives
To shower them with love and compassion
So they know they are never alone.

BEARING WITH EACH OTHER

Mom, Dad, and I are trying hard to be
Patient with each other, but
At times, we aren't.

Sometimes, our words to each other are harsh.
We're frightened of losing control.
We're frustrated when we can't have our way.
We're furious that everything is changing.

We're all trying.
We're all imperfect.
I'm wrong at times.
Mom and Dad are right at times.
We're all doing our best.

I must bear with them
As they must bear with me
As you, Lord, must bear with all of us.

Grant me compassion and understanding
So although I'm not elderly, I can see
The world through Mom's and Dad's eyes.

IN THE MIST

Soothe my aching heart, Lord,
When my parents' minds fade,
As memories are erased and the
Present slips away from them.

Comfort me when they are
Frightened by strangers and
Demons only they can see, when they
Talk to long-dead relatives.

Calm me when their words don't make sense,
When they are confused as I talk to them,
And they forget what I just said.

Guide me to enter their world so
They are not lost in the mist.
Give me slow and easy words that
Treat them respectfully as adults.

When they struggle to button a shirt,
Cut their meat, feed themselves,
Help me understand that they
Feel like children,
Embarrassed that they need help.

Make my actions
Quiet and unobtrusive
So their dignity is preserved.

Soothe me when they
Accuse others of stealing and
Me of locking them away,
Not caring about them.

Calm me when their frustration is
Disguised as anger because they
Feel helpless and miserable.

Lord, help me remember that
Angry, hurtful words are not them.
It's the excruciating pain
Of age speaking.

Guide me not to take their
Words personally or respond in anger.
Fill my heart with empathy
And my mouth with reassuring words
So they know they are safe,
Loved, and never alone.

Winter's Rewards

The gray skies and bare trees
Of winter remind me of aging.

The landscape looks bleak.
My heart is heavy with sadness.

Then you, Lord, light the sun to
Melt the ice that skims the pond.

You send a cardinal to
Sing outside the window.

You touch the moon and stars to
Shimmer on fresh snow.

In old age, it's easy to see only
The frailty of mind and body.

But you, Lord, show me the beauty of aging,
The soft gray hair that frames a pretty face.

The loveliness of a whispered
"I love you."

Their smiles and laughter
Around the dinner table.
The strong hands that
Can still clasp mine.

Now the sky is a brilliant blue.
The holly berries are cherry red.
Everything is brighter.
My heart is serene.

Prayer for Struggling Families

I pray for families who are
Struggling to care for elderly parents
While raising children and working.
Lord, give them strength.

Lord, relieve the burden of
Families who don't have
The financial resources to make
Caregiving less stressful.

I pray for families who argue about
How to care for aging parents
And need to agree on a way forward.
Lord, give them patience.

Lord, grant relief to the
One in each family who
Sacrifices and bears all the duties of
Caregiving alone.

I pray for people who can't
Face caregiving because
They are afraid of old age.
Lord, give them courage.

Lord, bless all caregivers
With your abundant grace.

A Heavy Burden

Oh, Lord, your yoke is not easy,
Nor is this burden light
For me or Mom and Dad.

It's hard to see them struggle
For words to express themselves
When once they came easily.

Upsetting to watch their minds
Grow more confused, thinking
Today is Christmas when it's the Fourth of July.

Painful to see their bodies
Stooped with age, their feet shuffle
When once they moved effortlessly and quickly.

Difficult to see food
Pushed aside when once they
Enjoyed their meals.

Heartbreaking to realize their eyesight
Has dimmed when once they
Loved to read.

Sad to see days filled
With doctors' appointments
Instead of enjoying the sunshine.

But you, Lord, know about
Yokes and burdens as you
Carried your cross to Calvary.

Lift us out of our pain and sorrow.
Carry this caregiving cross with us
So we can bear it with courage and strength.

THE LORD WAITS FOR ME

I wander, lost and afraid,
In the dense forest of caregiving.

No light, compass, or map
To guide me. Storms batter me.

Tears run down my cheeks as
Brambles cut, as tree roots trip me.

I stumble into a warm, dry cave where
You are waiting for me, Lord.

You say, *Rest awhile, tell me
Everything that makes you cry.*

How do I encourage Mom and Dad
To be as active as they can?

How do I help them make good decisions
For themselves when they are able?

How do I balance what they want
With what is best for them?

How do I maintain their dignity
When so much of their privacy is gone?

You nod in understanding,
Embrace me and promise me:

*I will answer each time you need me and
Give you the words so your parents understand.*

I will give you patience when yours runs out
And courage when you are afraid.

I will shower your heart with compassion to understand
Your parents' doubts and fears.

I will give you empathy for an
Old age you have not lived.

I will make you wise so you can
Guide them toward peace and happiness.

Sometimes you will think I am whispering
Because of the noise in your head.

Sometimes my voice will sound loud and clear
Because you are still.

Sometimes you won't remember I am with you
Because you are busy.

But times like these, when you rest,
You will feel my strong arms around you.

As I lean on your strong shoulder,
The rain stops, as do my tears.

COURAGE FOR MOM AND DAD

I see Mom and Dad's
Courage in physical therapy,
Patience with endless medical tests, and
Trust in others to help them.

They endure physical pain,
Emotional heartbreak as they
Long for their youthful strength and
Freedom to live as they want.

Ease their pain, Lord, when they
Suffer from all they've lost.
When more is asked of them,
Renew their spirits.

Encourage them so they can live
Each day as a blessing
To seek the strength that can
Only come from you.

A New Calling

Life is different now.
Days of freedom to
Do whatever I want:
Gone.

Time with friends, long walks
Through the woods,
Standing by the ocean:
Gone.

Friends ask,
"Did you see, hear?
Can you come?"
No, I didn't, and I'm sorry I can't.

I am exhausted, like roses that
Bloomed as long as they could,
Then dropped petals and withered away.

I am empty,
Like a hollowed-out ancient oak that
Lives but is struggling.

I need rain and sun
To refresh me into green growth
Like tender spring grass.

I miss the way I used to live.
I wish my new life was different,
But this is the life you've me called to, Lord.

Make me like the violet
Clematis that blossoms as it
Stretches to the cerulean sky.

HOPES AND DREAMS

When I look at the elderly,
Help me remember, Lord, that
They were just like me in their youth.

Bursting with energy,
Filled with hopes and dreams:
Some fulfilled, some not.

Help me recall the young and nurturing
Wife and mother, the strong and hardworking
Husband and father.

They laughed and cried,
Made mistakes, did their best,
Cared and sacrificed for me.

Their looks and lives are
Different now, but they
Are not empty shells.

Lord, help me remember even
When Mom's and Dad's behavior is
Childlike, they are still adults.

Help me focus not on what is lost, but
On the beauty, the simplicity of what
We have now.

IN MY OWN WORDS

Too often, I'm distracted and
In a hurry when I pray.

I sometimes pray with beautiful words
Others have written.

Often, they don't express
What I carry deep in my heart.

So I pray in my own words, Lord,
Even though they aren't always eloquent.

In these prayers, I unburden myself
Of the worry and pain that hurt my heart.

I beg forgiveness for my failures and
Ask for the help only you can give.

I praise your mighty power and
Thank you for your bountiful blessings.

I trust that you love me, Lord.
I trust that you hear my prayers.
I trust that you are always with me.

WHEN I AM GRATEFUL

TREASURE TIME TOGETHER

I'm grateful we are together to
Celebrate birthdays with
Chocolate cupcakes and
Rainbow sherbet.

To sit in the cool shade of the
Gazebo while a spring breeze
Ruffles daylilies as they
Dance in the sun.

To watch autumn leaves of
Gold, orange, and scarlet
Wave at us through a
Hospital window.

Even though Mom may drift off
To sleep during a visit or her
Mind may wander, she
Loves that I am with her.

Even though Dad barely
Touches his dinner or
Speaks, he has enjoyed
A great party with his family.

Lord, bless every visit with
Joy because only you know
Which one will be the last goodbye
Before you call Mom and Dad home to you.

THE GOOD DAYS

Lord, thank you for the days you
Lift Mom and Dad out of the
Doldrums of the waning days.

When Dad enjoys a hot dog and
His favorite ice cream because
He felt like eating.

When Mom strokes a puppy's
Soft brown ears because
His energy makes her feel alive.

When he remembers songs from
Childhood, delighted that his
Words come easily.

When she paints pink petals like
Cherry blossoms that flutter in
The spring, like our grateful hearts.

Thank you, Lord, for the times you
Bless Mom and Dad with brighter
Days and joyful hearts.

Kindness

Lord, thank you for the people who
Come into our lives when we
Need them most.

Bless the ones who hold doors
So I don't have to struggle
To get a wheelchair inside.

Bless the ones who don't
Honk their horns while I
Get Mom and Dad out of the car.

Bless the ones who stop to
Say hello when we are in
The dining room.

Bless the ones who bring
A flower from their garden
To brighten their apartment.

Bless the ones who are
Considerate, caring, and
Patient as we cope with old age.

HEARTS BEATING TOGETHER

Lord, thank you for patience
To repeat myself when Mom and Dad don't understand,
To listen to stories they must tell and retell,
Because they need someone to talk to.

Thank you for compassion to
Understand their fears,
Share their concerns,
Ease their loneliness.

I am grateful you are beside us
Sharing the sorrows and joys
Of the remaining days.

Most of all, Lord, thank you
For your trust in me and
my trust in you.

Help me always to
See through their eyes,
Relieve their pain,
Match my heartbeat with theirs.

STILL THEIR CHILDREN

No matter how old I grow,
Mom and Dad are still parents
Who can't stop nurturing.

Who worry I am doing
Too much, growing too tired.

Who want to give me half their
Dinner because they want me to eat more.

Who want to pay for my gasoline
Because I took them to the doctor.

Who will eat dessert
Only if I eat some too.

Lord, bless them for their
Care of me while I care for them.

REJOICE ALWAYS

When the sun shines and
The day runs smoothly,
I am grateful, Lord.

When there is time to do
Everything that needs to be done
And still have a few minutes for myself.

When no one is in the hospital,
Crying or confused,
I am grateful, Lord.

Thank you for strength that
Flows through me like
Sweetness through a maple tree.

For your love that
Embraces me like
Warm air on a spring day.

For the tranquility that
Pours over me like a
Cooling waterfall.

When the moon shines
At the end of a good day
For Mom, Dad, and me,
I give you thanks, my loving Lord.

SOMEONE TO LISTEN

Lord, bless the people who
Offer well-meaning advice
But don't understand a
Caregiver's challenges.

Help me listen patiently,
Reply gently, and ask them for
The help I need the most.

Someone to listen to my
Pain, doubts, and fears,
To cry with me.

Someone to listen and talk
About something other than
Caregiving for just a little while.

Someone to laugh with me,
To lighten the load so
I don't feel so alone.

Someone to pray for
Me and my loved ones.

Bless the someone,
Friend or stranger, Lord,
Who thinks of us often,
Who listens as we pour out our hearts to them.

BLESS ALL HANDS AND HEARTS

Bless the caregivers who work in hospitals and
Assisted living homes. Lord, they are your
Hands, eyes, ears, and voice
That relieve the suffering.

Bless those workers who
Care for frail bodies,
Listen to fears, dry tears, and
Soothe heartaches with a
Reassuring word and loving touch.

Bless those often overlooked who tirelessly
Clean the rooms, do the laundry,
Bring fresh linens, make the bed,
Bathe and dress our loved ones.

Bless them when they bring a cup of water,
Take our loved ones to recreation,
Prepare food and feed those
Who can't feed themselves.

Bless the caregivers with
Patience when the day is difficult, and
Strength when they are weary.

Bless them with the intuition to know
What the elderly need even when
Those in their care can't tell them.

Make us always ready to help and
Support caregivers, to be
Generous with our thanks and praise.
If we do find fault, make our words kind.

Lord, we are grateful for the
Caregivers who care for our
Loved ones as their own.

For Those Who Walk with Us

Abundantly bless our brothers
And sisters, Lord, who sacrifice and
Help us care for our parents.

Bless us with understanding to
Appreciate each other's point of view,
Disagree with respect, and
Work together in harmony.

Help us fairly divide the
Responsibilities for Mom and Dad
Based on our talents, abilities,
And other obligations.

Make us quick to listen,
Slow to criticize, and
Wise to understand that
Each of us is doing our best.

Remind us to thank each other often,
Appreciate each one's talents,
Acknowledge each one's fears, and
Support one another.

Thank you, Lord, for the gift of
Our brothers and sisters who
Share the joys and sorrows of caregiving.

For the One Who Stands by My Side

Thank you, Lord, for my husband
Who loves and supports me
As I care for Mom and Dad.

Bless him when he helps
At home, so I can
Rest when I'm exhausted.

When he listens to my fears,
Consoles me, and offers wise counsel.

Bless him when he reassures me
On the hardest days that
I'm doing a wonderful job.

Bless him for his gentleness and patience
With my mom and dad who are
Confused, lonely, and frightened.

Thank you for creating the
Thoughtful and generous man
Who helps without being asked and
Shares in all my trials.

Shower him with every grace
And blessing for standing
Steadfastly by me.

WHEN I NEED PEACE

MOVE MY MOUNTAIN

Caring for Mom and Dad
Feels like moving a mountain.
My faith feels smaller
Than a mustard seed.

Help me to pray often, especially
When I'm sad, tired, and distracted
Even if it's just to say,
"Lord, help me."

I know you've heard my imperfect prayers
When someone has a kind word,
When everyone is calm,
When my cross gets a little lighter.

I know you've heard me when I
Look up at the night sky and
See the slice of radiant moon
Like the winking of your eye.

I'm sure you've heard me when I
Watch the sun shine,
Warm and comforting,
Like the loving smile on your face.

I'm certain you've heard me because
Even though my faith is
Smaller than a mustard seed,
You tell me, *I, the Lord, will move your mountain.*

THE LORD IS ALWAYS WITH ME

Some days I walk in the
Sun's brilliance.

Some days I wander through the
Dense fog of desolation.

But when the noise of the day
Surrenders to the silence of the night,

You remind me, Lord, that you are
My refuge and my strength,

Always with me on the hardest days
And in the wakeful nights.

THE END IS NEAR

The end is near for Dad.
It is in the bend of his spine,
The hand that shakes as he
Searches for words to speak to me.

The end is near as Dad
Pushes away food and says
He is so tired before he
Slips off to sleep.

The end is near for Mom.
It is in her eyes that no longer sparkle,
Lips that rarely smile,
Skin as thin as parchment.

The end is near for Mom,
Who eats and speaks very little as
Her mind struggles to understand
And her frail body grows thinner.

I don't want them to go, but
Please, Lord, end their suffering.
Make their passage from this life
To the next swift, painless.

When it is time to leave this valley
Of tears, Lord, take them by the
Hand, lead them to heaven,
And give them rest.

HEAVEN'S PEACE

I wasn't with Dad when he
Slumped over and
Slipped from this life into an
Eternal one with an easy labor.

Now I pray that the mist which
Clouded Dad's mind drifts away,
That his beautiful mind is restored
And his words come easily once again.

I pray that his numb feet and legs are now strong,
The clear vision that eluded him most of his
Adult life is now his, and he can
See his wife and children from heaven.

Lord, I pray that Dad has
Found peace with you for all eternity.

THE LORD'S COMFORT

Mom suffers from loneliness,
Grieving for her husband
Who was her constant companion.

She is confined to a wheelchair
That she propels down
Empty halls to an empty room.

Please, Lord, give me words to
Console her, dry her tears, and
Fill her life with comfort.

When I cannot be there, Lord,
Wrap your loving arms around her
And ease Mom's sorrow.

Please, Lord, give her grace to
Bear with her suffering.
Otherwise, how will she endure it?

TRY FAITH

Mom cries because she misses Dad.
She asks why he had to die.
She wants a miracle, for him to
Sit beside her, healthy and alive.

Mom is hopeless.
I feel helpless.
I can't make this better.

Driving home, I see a license plate.
TRY FAITH, it says.

I blink in disbelief,
But the car is gone.
Did it really say TRY FAITH?

Please, Lord, let me see it again.
The car appears a mile later.
The plate doesn't say TRY FAITH.
It reads TRY F-A-T-H.

Why this curious spelling?
Maybe because perfectly spelled,
The message would be easy to forget.

Instead, I'm still pondering
These words, that I need to
Deepen and strengthen my faith
Because my help is in the name of the Lord.

ANGELS FOR MOM

I wasn't with Mom when the
Angels came at midnight to
Escort her, quietly,
Effortlessly to heaven.

I pray that the fog which
Robbed Mom of easily
Chatting with me is lifted and
Conversation becomes a joy.

I pray her hands that once beautifully
Arranged flowers are strong again,
That her creative mind that made holidays
And birthdays special is restored.

I pray that she can see her daughters
From heaven who are healthy, happy,
Who care for each other as she wanted.

I pray that Mom has found
Happiness with Dad and
You, Lord, in paradise forever.

REGRET

Dad died on a Tuesday.
A day when I was usually there.
But that morning, I wasn't.

Mom died on a Sunday
In the middle of the night.
I wasn't there.

Not that I could have saved them,
But I wanted to be there for them
Just one more time.

Lord, why did you take them when
I wasn't there, after I had been
With them so often for years?

Was it more peaceful,
Easier, better for them and me
Without a final goodbye?

WASH AWAY SORROW

Unrelenting sadness overpowers me
As I mourn, yearning for relief
From the sorrow gripping my heart.

Smother the flames of pain, Lord,
Lift me out of the powerful waters
Of grief where I am drowning.

Please send a sign that
Mom and Dad are safely
Home with you in heaven.

In the darkness, you
Sprinkle stars with one
Shining brighter than the others.

You send a bird I cannot
See to sing a joyful song
Among the rustling autumn leaves.

You wash away the sorrowful night,
Dry my tears like the sun
Kissing the morning dew.

I smile at the beauty Mom and Dad left behind
As you soothe my aching heart and
Reassure me that Mom and Dad are in your loving arms.

A Caregiver's Gratitude

True to your promise, Lord,
I believe you are always with me.

Thank you for your many blessings
and your bountiful love for me.

When my earthly life is done,
please bestow your mercy on this caregiver and
Grant me a place in heaven with you.

A Prayer to St. Jude
for the Elderly

I have a special devotion to St. Jude, who I pray to when I feel over-
whelmed and helpless. He is a powerful intercessor who always helps
me. I've written this prayer for you to insert your own intentions for
those you are praying for.

St. Jude, patron saint of hopeless cases
And impossible situations,
Please pray for the elderly who
Face pain, loneliness, and the
Acute awareness that their
Time on earth is coming to an end.

I ask your powerful intercession
For (name your special intention).
Ask God to lift their spirits,
Ease their suffering, and
Bless their passing from this life to the next
As he welcomes them home to heaven.

St. Jude, I pray for all
Caregivers, children of the elderly,
And spouses who feel overwhelmed,
Alone, and exhausted caring for the elderly.
Please intercede for (name your special intention).
Ask God to comfort, support, and
Guide all caregivers.

Thank you, St. Jude, for
Listening to my prayer.

About the Author

Abundant Strength: A Caregiver's Prayers is Lynn H. Wyvill's second book of poetry, a heartfelt personal reflection on her time caring for her elderly parents. Her first book, *Nature's Quiet Wisdom*, is a collection of poetry that invites the reader to walk nature's path to find the wisdom residing there. Lynn started her career as a radio and TV reporter, producer and writer, and then opened her business as a corporate communications trainer. After a long search for a new way to express herself, she discovered the joy of writing. Lynn finds inspiration in nature and all that surrounds her. She is a lifelong learner, curious about the world, and lives in beautiful Virginia with her artist husband.

Connect with the Author

lynnhwyvill.com
facebook.com/lynnhwyvill
instagram.com/lynnhwyvill

Leave a Review

If you enjoyed *Abundant Strength: A Caregiver's Prayers*, will you consider writing a review on your platform of choice? Reviews help indie authors find more readers like you.

Made in the USA
Middletown, DE
18 September 2022

10729988R00066